MW00982148

Active Pass

Jane Munro

Active Pass

PEDLAR PRESS | TORONTO

COPYRIGHT © 2010 Jane Munro

ALL RIGHTS RESERVED. No part of this book
may be reproduced or transmitted in any form or by
any means whatsoever without written permission
from the publisher, except by a reviewer, who may
quote brief passages in a review. For information,
write Pedlar Press at PO Box 26, Station P, Toronto
Ontario M5S 2S6 Canada.

ACKNOWLEDGEMENTS
The publisher wishes to thank the Canada Council
for the Arts and the Ontario Arts Council for their
generous support of our publishing program.

LIBRARY AND ARCHIVES CANADA
CATALOGUING IN PUBLICATION

Munro, Jane, 1943-
    Active pass / Jane Munro.

ISBN 978-1-897141-38-0

    I. Title.

PS8576.U574A67 2010   C811'.54
C2010-904110-0

EDITED FOR THE PRESS by Roo Borson

COVER ART *Fish Head in Steel Sink* by Mary Pratt,
courtesy of the artist

DESIGN Zab Design & Typography, Toronto

TYPEFACE Bembo

Printed in Canada

for Roo

When no one is present,

but it appears that someone is present,

autumn is here.

— ROO BORSON, "Autumn Record"

.

CONTENTS

Active Pass

Mary Pratt: Illuminations

Nearer Prayer than Story

ACTIVE PASS

Midway on its crossing from Tsawwassen to Swartz Bay, the ferry enters Active Pass, a scenic but dangerous strait where visibility is limited, currents vigorous, and vessels alter course.

1

We live where night seeps straight down—
wine on the wicks of stars.

A rock carved by waves and warmed by sun
that's easy to sit in. A lap. A body to lean on.

I'm a little deafened by the constant breaking
of the ocean. Change, change, change—

but what has it learned? Throwing itself against stones.
Rounding them up. Scotch bottle broken and rolling.

My father softened as beach glass—
ground down.

2

The doe's head points away from the road.
Dying, she surged out of herself, aiming for the bush.

Two ravens hopping on gravel scold me.
Jogging past daily, I track her disintegration.

My father in my arms, remarkably heavy.
I thought ashes were light.

The first day, her head is intact. Eyelashes.
The ravens are bloodying her, but she still has fullness.

No hot flashes, but I freeze. Yesterday, gloves
for typing. Yes, in July. No kidding.

They unwrap her chest and hips. Her middle
is hollow. Long white thigh bones. Socks of fur.

3

Drawing salary out of hours. Fur
combed from a mongrel's back, carded, spun.

Emergency Road Service wedged open a window,
fed in a tape with a Velcro loop, caught the lock button.

Ambulance driver gave me a quarter and a phone number.
Searching for my notes in the elevator.

Lesson time: why did I lose touch?
My drive. My keys. My mobility. My wits.

The quietness of creatures sizing up danger.
Could I hold that still?

Even when I shed work, its presence clings.
Dog loyal, that's it. Protected by my stinking sweater.

4

At the bottom of the well, a hermit crab.
The object he gave me: a turtle's carapace.

When I asked him what to do, he said: "It's not a job
problem, it's a *sturm und drang* problem."

House on my back. Neck out.
Gunnery practice across the strait. Thuds

at the pace of heartbeats. What I want now
is not what a woman wants from a man.

I want what an egg wants from its DNA.
I want this with all the greed of a grub.

5

Mistress Quickly feeling Falstaff's feet. Hal on horseback,
"I know you not." Myself, a shock and a betrayal.

I fight exhaustion all week. In Oporto we ate quail's eggs:
tiny, speckled, sepia orbs. I wore a red t-shirt.

Ale and laughter in the taproom below. "Well, dear—
goodbye for now." My father's last words to me.

The man interred not only in my DNA
but in my turn of phrase, my taste.

And my dark hair. It turned wavy—long and thick—
when I was pregnant. Pushing a stroller in a sage jumpsuit.

6

Waiting for the phone to ring. Jelly bag
hung in the doorway. Full of crushed blueberries.

Like a soul between life-times, un-reincarnated,
afloat on radio waves. A river of piano notes.

"The Big Bang's a bust," says an expert on *Ideas*.
No call. Not short-listed. Not wanted locally.

Even my bedding plants won't grow.
Thumb-high marigolds. Minute snapdragons.

The indigo of mussel shells. Salal berries. Stellar's Jays
drumming on the metallic handles of the wheelbarrow.

Fall rye sown across a new septic field.
Flash of blue against sword ferns.

So, I'm cast to the birds. Flicker on a spruce
lifting scabs of bark. Its head a fierce drill.

7

Sturgeon, unchanged for three million years, washed up.
A giant's white slippers, tangled in low branches.

Gilled dinosaurs. Surviving ice age, continental drift, grizzlies.
We've slain the giant. Turned its river into a drain.

Already, the wired-tired state. One day back
and I'm into it. Sleep: the water my mind leap-frogs.

I remember deep sedge, waving willows,
stream's edge, dreaming.

"Ghosts in the river," the radio called them. Marking time.
Nineteen-hour days. Swirling hallways. Deciduous names.

8

My father's doctor shook hands. "Pneumonia,
friend of the elderly." Told us he'd met an easy death.

The mice made a nest of moss in the woodpile.
It looked like a muff, big enough for two hands.

I pleaded for a muff like Katrina's,
the storybook skater. "No sirree!" my mother said.

"Your hands would be stuck." In intensive care,
they paralyzed her. She was fighting the respirator.

Stroking her forehead and singing, "Skeeters
am a-humming," and "There's a long, long trail a-winding."

If only I could have held his hand. Hers puffed up,
but the touch—our touch—lasts.

9

The kitchen has a built-in ironing board,
and copper pennies dropped by former tenants

between the stove and fridge. I circulate
in hallways. Mail box. Laundry. Garbage.

Ferries split the week. Nights in a pumpkin shell.
Where would I wander? Now, all I crave is solitude.

Alarm clocks ring. Radiators percolate.
The building hums. A dryer turns over its load.

Residents. Towels. Shorts.
City blocks under unsorted clouds. I carve

a jack-o-lantern: strings of slimy goop laden with seeds
like fake fingernails. My arm, sticky to the elbow.

10

A boogie man's bagged me in a tar-pungent sack.
He ups his pace. I'm thump-thumping against his back.

"Don't let your imagination run away with you!"
she warned. As if I'd chosen.

On the ferry, I see a white-haired woman
and cry. All my wise ones, my contradictors, have died.

A racket on the beach: stones losing every edge.
Pebbles sucked up. Flung down. Sunday's sighs.

The week's urgent attack. Bursting file folders.
Cuticles torn. Coffee beans in the glove compartment.

Waking in hot water.
I thought his death would be easier than hers.

11

Switchbacks. Vista east, coming over the Malahat.
Row of peaks across the water. Then, a grid of vines.

She lifts the glass pipette from a carafe and slips
one amber drop onto the back of my hand.

I expect a blessing: "preserve you in eternal life."
Suck it up while noticing my knuckles.

A vintage boiled, evaporated, casqued, bottled.
Residue of champagne. Now vinegar.

Driving the twisting road home,
my mouth an echo chamber for bitter ethers.

12

Where the ground's disturbed, orange fungus.
Mouths of goldfish. Puckered lips.

Chain of paper dolls. Linked like mushrooms.
I've cut a folding stack: my selves, a history.

She lectured me, "You'll never be beautiful,
but you can always be nice."

I recall human fat—pale, dimpled—
in a jar on a shelf in St. Paul's hospital.

So what's left to eat? Iceberg lettuce?
Death's keel my stabilizer.

13

Men don't ache like this—don't tighten wires
lumbar to sacrum, clench hips and pubis.

Bull Kelp—the fastest-growing annual—pumps out
forty metres in six months. Holdfast, stipe, blades, spores.

Loops of the strait's intestines
heaped on the beach.

Ashes and seaweed to the compost. His whistle.
Onboard, the tinned salmon sandwich tastes of margarine.

A jet stream nicknamed the Pineapple Express.
Boxcars of lows: Progestin. Estrogen. F.S.H.

14

My hands are changing: no more blank skin—
palms cross-hatched, veins bulging,

fingers flushed or withered. Weeknights I eat
crackers and cheese and drink Chilean wine.

Fall asleep in blue sheets faded from many washings.
Another funeral today. My model couple sails away

across the galaxy in a Lightning. They tent
on island shores along the Milky Way.

To keep exhaustion at bay, I make eye contact.
Into old age, those two climbed a new peak each year.

15

Our grey cat noses open the cellar door.
Hung from his jaw, a bunny—brown, floppy.

When he eats shrews, he crunches their small bones
and purrs. Then, hunkers on my lap.

Warm snoozing creature beneath the newspaper.
Its headline: "Rwanda's Gory History."

A man on a Rockhound harrows the meadow,
gathering stones from Earth's larder.

16

I grew up in an unfinished house. Learning to brace
against hammering. Holding walls in place.

Gum erasers and tracing paper.
Great T-square on a green drawing board.

In the end, he overflowed allocated space.
Broke chairs. Now I have a huge investment

in death. Sense him
nested in my mother. The jar of his ashes

we placed in her grave. His snores. Scratched glasses.
Scientific American. Crosswords. Rhododendron blooms.

17

I forgot my clothes! No suitcase. No skirt. No sweater.
No power this morning. Bleeding. But, no excuse.

Mind like a pussy willow, texture of a catkin.
Yesterday, grey nubbins, engorged raindrops.

Swags of mist drifting in and out of the forest.
There were years when I couldn't shower alone,

carried babies front and back. Now, I study stones—
how old they are! How sleek and round.

Off to the second-hand store. Off with jeans
I've worn for three days. Get me spring colours.

18

Shu'ua tells the cops, "If you shoot him,
do it with his shirt on."

They'd followed him into her shack.
They figured they had him cornered.

He'd come at me with an ice pick.
But even in handcuffs, he's sweet-talking her.

They're both in the all-together, she with one breast
longer than the other. She swaths herself in a bolt

of white tulle; he slips his shirt on.
It perfectly matches what's behind him—

skyline of mountains, salmonberry bush. He disappears.
She's married the land; the land will stay with her.

Shu'ua tells me, "It's not about you."
Fine. But, she's in my dream.

19

I develop a technique for unlocking doors one-handed.
Always carrying too much stuff.

Ten months after my father's death,
he has loosened fifty years from his frame.

A doubled spruce. Salt air in blasts. Candles on the table.
Your calls. Your voices. Asters. House wren.

A bird's flight through the banquet hall.
Out the other door. Gust of cold.

What I didn't know was closed begins to open.
A small wind pushes the heart ajar.

Is it this simple? In the lap of a boulder, a pool
of salt water. Maroon sea star's rough skin.

20

Mt. Baker sliced by telephone lines. The Fraser delta
waterlogged. Driving Highway 10, laid straight out

past horses in muddy paddocks. Poles and wires.
Mountains in a sun break up the valley—Golden Ears

to the north. Draining from the Fraser's mouth,
a plume of brown. The shock of horse power:

in Siena, at Palio, pressed against temporary fencing—
inches from steaming flanks, streaming tails—

bareback riders six abreast at the top of the track
churning by—pounding into yesterday.

A year of patience, a friend called it. When exhausted,
do not start anything. No recriminations. No fixes.

A year in the compost bin. When mud floods you.
When your outlook's cut to bits.

21

Going home with five plastic bags of chicken shit
for the garden we're starting from scratch.

Going home—up the gravel drive beyond street lights,
municipal water, or garbage collection.

Mother read Bahá'í texts while smoking on the toilet.
Toyota station wagon's my confessional.

After little islands, the big one. I can smell the Pacific.
Feel my cheek on your chest.

MARY PRATT: ILLUMINATIONS

*Dreaming while still awake is something I do with expert
and long-standing ability.*

— MARY PRATT

Winter Solstice: Vancouver

Parking across the street, just before the bridge,
I can see them: portraits of persimmon,
apple, peach, watermelon and lemon
in the front window of the Equinox Gallery.
And inside, another: green grapes lustrous as roe,
piled off-centre on a plate of galactic garnet glass.
Upstairs, her painting of a dead robin
on weathered planks. Even the wood's grain is feathered.
Is falling in love with art, falling for make-believe?
In Konya, in Rumi's twelfth-century madressa,
I saw a reflecting pool under an open dome
where Sufis measured the flow of stars. I wanted
to read constellations printed on that sheet of water.
Falling in love with art makes me believe.

Eggs in Egg Crate

You see an open papier mâché egg crate
in the middle of her painting—a dozen moulded cups
and tray-like lid. The crate's half-filled
with egg shells, their tops and bottoms nested.
Pratt's painted it in skin tones: ivory, cream,
ochre, amber, rust. It's a study of light
absorbed by porous cardboard, waxy on shells.
But it's the crate's shadow that faces us.
Realism reminiscent of a women's magazine—
food porn—though here there is no pretty dish.
The omelette's made; breakfast's over.
We see spent shells, ready to be tossed. Their box,
soon closed. Her title's tongue-in-cheek. This is not
a painting of eggs. She's depicted empties.

In a year of the video-taped, naked Kate Craig
as "Lady Brute," slipping on and off a leopard-spotted vest—
of Gathie Falk's galloping "Herd One" (carousel troop
of plywood ponies bounding across gallery floors)—
of two stone masks reunited (one with eyes closed,
one with eyes open), a cupped pair carved for an ancient
Tsimshian nax nox dancer—in the year after Evelyn Roth
knit Vancouver's Art Gallery an awning of videotape
and Mr. Peanut ran for mayor—in the International
Women's Year, in the time of Judy Chicago's "Dinner Party,"
Pratt chose to paint a housewife's trash. To pass
as an ordinary woman. Yet her plain art spins
heart's sprockets like a love letter from your kitchen.
On the counter: an original, conceptual, happening.

So—where did the eggs go? Into a batter
for a birthday cake? Or, did the artist—
not the mother—separate them?
Toss a yolk from palm to palm, pinch up
the drooping globe and prick it
over powdered pigment, add water. Either way,
the eggs have made an appearance. Pratt didn't mean
her tricks to show; it's ours she's after.
As if she'd fasted, spread red plaster
on a wooden panel, gessoed that, then stencilled in
a holy icon—divining her subject. Coloured it to code
with sable brushes. Breath by breath,
adhered each flake of gold. Made a power
to enter mind, and from inside, reveal us to us.

Puddle of egg white left in each, as if the cook
were moving too fast to scoop out the last dollop
with her finger. Cardboard sockets holding shells.
Six used. Six ova implicit in Pratt's six children.
Four fed and sent to school. Then, a decade later, twins
lost in late term, the year she painted this.
Is the little life, the almost-life, before birth…useful?
The unseen sensed: kicking you from inside.
For years I dreamt of babies I would not conceive,
had chosen to forgo, lined up in bassinettes.
I saw each infant's sleeping face, and grieved.
Pratt's image a matrix
of mystery: cups cupping cups. Plenty.
Then, lickety-split, naught.

Girl in a Wicker Chair

Without a stitch on. Perched in a wicker armchair.
Wary. Legs drawn up, knees to chin. Feet splayed
on seat's edge. Toes bumpy—the most uneven parts
of her. She's symmetrical. Glazed. Almost, a porcelain
figurine: lustrous body, sleek dark hair. The wing chair
is capacious—woven and airy—her uncurling calyx.
In its middle, her legs frame a shape like a vulva's
double-headed axe (or is it a tulip's chalice?) that strikes
all four focal points of the painting. Within the gap between
touching ankles and pressed-together shins, the inner curves
of thighs describe an hour-glass stem. Its upper goblet lit;
lower root-bulb, shadowed. Folded, her limbs are rounded:
firm as a green shoot. Compact as a spring. Neck tense. Jaw
squared. Perfect lips. Midnight stare. Moth in a split chrysalis.

The model's work is to sit—in the nude—for the artist
who sees her as his muse. The wife's work is to reproduce
the slide her husband took. Grasp what he fell for. Picture
this mirrored voyeurism, twisted as the wicker of the chair.
White-washed, too—this is no minx—she's too composed.
Glossy as a centrefold. Mary Pratt has this mapped, astute
as an archaeologist gazing at rolling pasture and pointing
to tumuli, a Lydian amphitheatre. Laying out her dig. Goats
may graze the surface, but those buried forms cast shadows.
Pratt reads the unexcavated. Probes her husband's unused
photographs of a naked woman he liked to paint. "Ma
Donna," his archetypal portrait. But it's flat. Matte. Mary
paints what he did not, unearthing the lovely Donna studying
him. Their model, their monument: Delphic domestic sphinx.

Donna watches us with shadowed eyes as an owl
might pause on a branch before unfurling doubly feathered
wings and dropping on its prey. Light rakes the surface—
tawny on the floor, amphibian on the wall, milk-toothed
against her skin. Wicker casts a lacy shadow. Creases
wilt the cushion's cotton cover, like a pillowcase slept on
all night. Cool hues. Smoothly parted hair hoods her erect
head. Hermaphrodite—female subject in a male structure
(stacked balls, shaft, glans)—which, at a glance, looks
lunar. Almost circular. A satellite. Donna as Diana.
Or Artemis, Apollo's twin, filling her gaze by watching him.
If this painting is Mary's first stab at the female nude, is it
also a self-portrait? She his artistic midwife. His first muse.
Now huntress: and we're in her grip on a moon-lit flight.

The Service Station

You've seen it before—three and a half centuries ago
Rembrandt painted "The Carcass of an Ox"
with a woman behind it, mopping up blood
pooling on the floor. But this is a new world corpse:
moose, headless, ribs and forelegs strung up on a crossbar,
hung from a hook on the back of her neighbour's
tow-truck, parked in his cement block garage—
a few flattened cartons spread on polished concrete to absorb
what's left of this wilderness cow, galloping off
with that camel-like gait: a rocking-up-jutting-hippy commotion,
until shot—stumbling—where the man
with the tow-truck could drag his prize out of the bush
and into this service station, hoisting her body as provision—
carving her up for roasts and stews.

Spread in a wide V—cloven hooves pointing up,
booted in velvet and lashed to a wooden beam.
An old lust. The bush his proving ground. His vehicle.
His station. Her bounty at his service. Don't think
he's messy. For a guy, he's tidy—maybe rushed,
but practical. He's done this before. You might count on him
to fix an engine. As a neighbour, he'd drop by with meat
for your freezer. You'd wrap it in pink butcher's paper,
or saran, or foil—whatever you normally use.
Men in white aprons. Sawdust. Wooden tables.
Cleavers in leather holders on the wall. But this raw garage
is not Mr. Sweed's butcher shop. Pratt's technique
is immaculate. Scentless. Finished with fine brushes.
Yet from the stem of your brain, a gagging stench.

Child with Two Adults

The baby's gaze is puzzled and downcast—directed at a foot
she's raised, glazed in bathwater, making a splash. The baby's
fists are tight—like a fighter's, up to parry or jab. One heel's
pressed against the side of the mixing bowl—her bath tub.
But it's that kicked foot—the same firm little foot that jutted
against uterine wall—she's eyeing. "Hello, Peanut!" Does she
recognize those voices? Air cools her thigh. A cloth licks
her side—what does she tell herself? It's clear, she's intent
on figuring this out. Wordless, but strenuously thinking.
Training her mind to pick out differences: what glitters,
slips, resists. Get a leash on hands and feet. Deliberate
on sound, smell, taste. Repeat fleet feelings. Make sense
of resonance. Envision herself as a body—one who can kick.
Notice how it happens. Find her edges. Discover patterns.

Three arms and hands reach into the basin to bathe her.
She's smack in the middle, centred: we look down on her.
Like us, she doesn't know who's there, or even
that two adults are caring for her. A shadowy cloud of hair
upper left: her mother? One of the woman's hands holding
the baby's head, the other dipped in water. Is that her father's
arm coming in lower right? Picking up a flannel, wrist
resting on the pottery rim. Bowl cracked but fine. Trimmed
with an interlocking chain. Behind, an heirloom linen cover—
perhaps a pillowcase. Is that their bed? The baby can't imagine
them as makers, what hands can craft, how they'll shape her.
When my mother died her friend told me, "Like a gardener
you can't see, she'll help you grow better." How familiar we are
with mystery! The child—slowly, slowly—becoming herself.

Blue Bath Water

By now it's clear: nothing's accidental. Pratt may paint
from a photograph, but she's patient and exacting, choosing
and composing every detail. So, why dye the bathwater blue?
Cobalt as a midnight sky in a northern summer.
It doesn't hide the woman in the tub. She's making waves
in all three inches of water, kicking up turbulence—a wake
of froth about her right hand and left foot. Playing
privately. Her breasts as firmly rounded as the tub's lip.
Enclosed in a lozenge with snips of rainbows. Candy skin
risen in ranges from an inland sea. Model. Ship in a bottle.
Light torches her body and the tub's curves. Touches her.
A Venus, out of the blue. Where does beauty come from?
Womb red walls and floor. Where will it go? She's kinetic—
nucleus of a cell in a bloodstream: scripted image. Genetic.

But, faceless. Head turned. Glorified in a full-body corona:
the gilded bathtub. Stretched out in sapphire water—
fishy virgin in a Vesica Piscis. Instead of a halo,
a mop of brown locks. Swivelling, averted from the public.
Pubic hair drenched with indigo: X marks the spot
in the middle of the picture. They say, indigo
causes sterility in the Bengali women who churn it.
When the devils and angels churned the sea,
first a poison arose—the draught Shiva swallowed,
turning his throat blue: sign of divine protection.
Later, the lovely Meenakshi swallowed Shiva's penis,
became his shakti: the fish-eyed goddess
who kept on dancing, undaunted by his show-off tricks,
outlasting him. Like cobalt's isotopes, sapphire's crystals.

Salmon between Two Sinks

Gutted. Fresh. Its eye still bright. Hooked mouth open
above one of the stainless steel sinks filled with water.
Tail not in the picture though it tips the fish.
Suspended on the divider between creature and meal.
Between visible and invisible. The image a triangle
like a marriage with a third party on which the body
gets hung up. A kind of pun. And yes, a fishy trinity.
Light falls in stripes through Venetian blinds
onto the salmon and the sink itself—metallic,
not attached to what goes on within it.
Like life. Like death. Silver scales stretched
over crimson flesh. The gape of gills.
Dependent drape of slashed belly: labial slit.
Food. God. Sex. It slips. Sticks. Works like a dream.

Burning the Rhododendron

The rhododendron grew huge, took up half the yard.
Teetering cones of purple blooms festooned it more solidly
than a department store's Christmas tree. As if a bevy
of elves worked in its gloom, packing up boxes
for the girls and boys who held their breath until once again
a magical train emerged from its branches, burdened with gifts.
The house lit with amethyst, corners softened, lavender
beside the bed. Vases of unstinting spring on the hearth.
When branches turned dry and grey, he pruned.
When roots clogged drains, they paid experts to unplug them.
She poured minerals around the drip line
to feed leaves mottled yellow, curling brown.
But in every storm, more of it shattered. They bound
cracked boughs, propped up the trunk. Consulted. Prayed.

One day, he walked in and told her the time had come.
They had to cut it down. Pile its limbs on a pyre.
Kindle them. See this fire—fierce as a sunspot—
erupt with sprays of sparks, flaming gas, fountains
white at the core then yellow, orange, burgundy, black—
the night carrying its waving flag—northern lights—ghosts
of all their springs filled with bowls of purple
rhododendron blooms. When I die, may my bones burn
with such a blaze. Yours too. May the bonfire
suck in all we ever knew—each day's light, your skin
after swimming, late laughter on the back step,
sheets stripped from a rumpled bed tossed high—lightning—
a fire equal to our loss, as is this wild burning
of the rhododendron in my heart.

Reflections of the Florentine in the Salmonier

What you see is a silver tea tray loaded with a china tea set
in front of an aquarium—which mirrors
cups and saucers and the landscape behind you:
tree trunks, grass, a hedge beyond the lawn at your back.
There's also one fish, pinkish, a fingerling,
more blurred than the reflections of the china
or the bubbles. You can tell it's afternoon by the shape
of the shadow close to the base of the teapot.
Wedgwood's Florentine: cobalt border embossed
with white swirls you realize are winged dragons,
griffins, crested urns, skulls of bulls crowned with suns,
burst rinds of pods, twisted and shooting plants.
Edged with a chain of eggs and crosses.
Until you look closely, you'd think nothing's happening.

Guests at my first wedding gave us the sister pattern—
Florentine Turquoise—with a lighter border and nosegay
of fruit at its centre. It reminds me of the blue and white
plastic tea set, left in its display case in the snow
by the door that Christmas we spent in the unfinished house.
Mother questioned the woman at the post office who knew
everyone, but couldn't find out whom to thank. Defiantly,
I liked to play with that tea set, arranging it on a stump, filling
the pot with water, pouring from its curved spout into cups,
pretending I had guests and we were deep in conversation.
In Pratt's painting, you see light playing on the glazed china—
a splotch of rose on the middle cup echoes the fish's pink.
As you look, it becomes a much-reduced image of a woman.
She's wearing something red, maybe a sweater. Like me.

Green Grapes and Wedding Presents with Half a Cantaloupe

A split cantaloupe's scooped-out cup and rough rind
held in a silver bowl with a fluted rim
over which is draped a stem of green grapes.
The bowl, brim-full with reflections,
sits on an oval platter. Has Pratt devised
its cobalt border to pass as Florentine? A goddess
in the orbit of another god urges alarmed horses
into tumult, through waves. The ivory platter's bruised
by echoes of the silver bowl in sunset light.
The painting's galactic—a spiral in composition.
Round and round their course the two
pursue each other. At its core, slick and shadowed
cantaloupe flesh—rosy melon, ripe and ready
for the spoon. Such delicious fruit. There, to be eaten.

Mary Pratt's Painting in the Equinox Gallery

A robin, fallen on wood planking.
A small painting—a study. Its feet up.
Its red breast an egg of luminous tufts:
all the variations performed by red—red's
repertoire of hues, of tints and shades.
And then the tail: blue, white and grey—
staves bundled for effective flight.
A yellow bill, closed eye, and smudge
emerging from the brain, as thought
waves might—a song escaping
into the wood's feathered grain.
There, a reflection of the bird—
flushed—entailed in the weathered decking.
A portrait of the soul departing.

NEARER PRAYER THAN STORY

Poems are nearer to prayers than to stories....
— JOHN BERGER

The quiet way to the happy country

From here to the grain elevator
is a long mile. I learned it by walking through dusk,
past young wheat, past Wolverine Creek
where a blue fog lay, thin
as a snake's skin, shed by the stream—
grown plumper from rain and meandering.
As the soul's foot is love,
we strolled there together, drawn to the tower
where seeds are stored. How many thousands—
stripped, winnowed, dried—were lodged inside?
Sleep gathered the mile, wound it up.
In the morning, a train unrolled it again—its whistle
the twisted paper ribbon of a gift ball
an aunt sent me from Rome:
as I pulled, sugared almonds fell out, silver jacks.
A scarf unfurled. At its centre, wrapped in tissue,
a locket. Whose picture goes in it?

That empty house, your heart

open as a house with all its doors ajar, hot
July night, a fan in the room
across the hall, earlier a few blinds rattled
but now there's no breeze
and even in the dark the heat builds

its own house—architect, carpenter—all
the trades under its belt—in your bed,
hair lifted, bare neck on cotton pillow slip, sheetless—
heat leads you, solders you—you are a fixture
heat incorporates like an awkward tub

enclosing you in a brocade drop-cloth
while it lifts walls, vaporizes ceilings, strips veins—
heart surgeon, saws studs apart, spreads
the frame with its fingers, slows its pulsing—
then brings in trees, a city park with swings,

cinnamon rolls with brown sugar and raisins,
the ancestor who gave you knock knees, and plaster
like a baby's skin, olive and rose—the clink of milk
bottles on the doorstep, throats of cream, and
a screen door by sweet peas—heat tiles the past

in a plush mosaic, turns the tap on full bore—
you're in an ocean, swimming with whales,
doors angled like fins, hall limpid with jellyfish
in spiralling constellations—fan futile, heat's
vast and naked and is gathering you in its wave

Delight in solitude

Near the Lady Shrine,

bolts of birdsong unfurl on the breeze.

Light as net curtains. Bird shadows fall:

hands on the shrine's housing. Wings

pulse past my ear—whirr, thrum.

What a fabric, this atmosphere!

Across its gable someone's painted:

Hail Queen of Peace!

In the end my Immaculate Heart will triumph.

The little mother stands inside amidst

plastic flowers, her eyes like doll's eyes—bright

and clear, set in the pale plaster of her face.

She's crowned, robed, bears an orb, wears a cross.

Airing the kitchen, my mother would open

casements and her yellow curtains

would tussle with their frames and float out

like spinnakers. But her real shrine

was the bathroom. Each morning

she'd carry in a little red book

and a cigarette, then sit

for twelve minutes behind a locked door.

When I came in, its plain pebbled window

would be agape. Tobacco smoke, toothpaste,

the hemp-soap smell of father's shaving bowl,

and a murky composted scent were the incense
for her meditation. A rush of damp air
blew in through the huckleberry bush
whose fingertip leaves held beads of rain.

I'd build shrines along the creek—
pile smooth stones in a bower, add
a robin's eggshell, salal berries, fir cones.
I'd wade in the stream, sing made-up songs,
and lay out my choice of wondrous things,
never quite clear who they were for.
The vine maples whose smooth springy trunks
hung over the water were perfect for bouncing on,
or sitting and swinging. Forest filled the canyon.
Other creatures—from skater-bugs to bears—
were at home there. I came to be happy.

As a merchant breaks in a fine horse, master yourself

Black cow crashing into the chute, bucking
so the metal hoists
off the ground, her weight tipping
forward, head thrust
through the front gates, locked
into this narrow
contraption—flinging strings of saliva,
spinning thick splattering ropes
carried by the wind
to hit the woman in overalls holding
a hypodermic, loaded with anthrax spore vaccine,
the man kneeling with a blue halter
he's dropped over her ears—she's now
down on the grass, glassy eyes bulging, heels
kicking out one side of the chute—he's
sliding the loop over her snout, but she bites
on it and he has to unhook
it from her mouth, getting slimy and soaked
but doing it calmly, adeptly.
We're perched on the tailgate of a truck,
a safe distance in case she breaks out.
He pierces the loose skin of her brisket
and inserts a sturdy loop, bends its ends
to secure a yellow tag—218—the number
his ten-year-old daughter beside me records

in a scribbler by the cow's birth date
and the code on the red button inside her ear—
a sequence he has to read, calling it off
in chunks as she bucks and froths,
before they can inoculate her, before
he takes his pliers to that dangly
bit of skin above her chest. The morning
warming up, but the wind still carrying
saliva our way, saliva and dust
and the smell of undigested
grass. She shits, pisses, and some of it hits
the woman in overalls, but then they're done.
Carefully, he lifts off the halter. They stand
back from the gate. He hauls on its lever. It opens
and she's out, galloping into the pasture, flicking her tail.

Give thanks

as I run, the rooms
come clear—I recall
narrow, creaking stairs,
their front hall and telephone,
my son's guitar upon its stand,
their yellow couch, tall kitchen cupboards—
a row of postcards on the doors—
his wife's computer, her leather jacket

then I come to
my older daughter's house
morning sun on its wooden floors—
the Whale Étude, blue dishes on the table,
a green duvet, white bassinette—
the linen closet I helped fill,
glass doors onto the deck—
sandbox, balls, a dump truck

next, I see my younger daughter
and her fellow, smell a latte brewing,
see stacks of books and papers,
her rumpled afghan on the sofa, a bike helmet—
hear traffic from the street below

finally, I come to our home—
today, you're sitting at the kitchen table,
looking up, expecting me—
not that I've a lot to say:
a road report, weather news—
I see a new tarp on the greenhouse roof,
the toppled foxglove in the front garden—
and tabbies curled on our bed
like twins in utero

molecules passing in and out of muscle cells—
all of us—fleet family—your rooms in my heart

You have no name and no form

The old wear thin.
It's possible
to see through him
into the blue his eyes frame
and let into the room.

He's light now—
a garden rake left leaning
against a trestle table. "I'd have liked
a last conversation...."

He's taking long strides
with the wind across grassland, catching up
to a further figure—
his heart bounding ahead.
When his friend notices and turns to wave,
he waves back.
The rolling plain is dancing.

If you cannot quieten yourself, what will you ever learn?

no one comes to this house, but the grasses sway
seed heads wave across the kitchen window
I am not alone—the wind is my guest

sitting up, spine erect—a ground squirrel
with thirteen stripes on her side
turns her head at the chickadee's voice
eye shiny as a watermelon seed
front paws hold a peanut while she chews
she dug a new entrance to her burrow
after I'd found the one under the bench
and began leaving treats: bits of apple
and carrot, raw nuts and seeds

above the creek, coyote cubs
lick each other's ears
their laughter
at the first tickle of a train—
they always hear it before me

window on a storm lasting half the night:
twitching brilliance under clouds
like fluorescent lights flicked on and off

momentarily
ploughed earth bleached, fields blanched
light yanked by its bare roots
from a furrowed sky

after the storm
an opaqueness
in my head—what a complex mess
we're in, and in me
what moves is sadness

though it's dark, I enter the woods
and follow a path, walking swiftly
believing it will take me
to the other side
only when I come out
exactly where I went in
do I realize the trail's a loop

an egg: its golden yolk
this small, quiet room
sections of orange
and more milky coffee—
mine for a while

if I go back
to a time before talk
will I find myself
in meditation?

no one comes to this house, but the grasses sway
seed heads wave across the kitchen window
I am not alone—the wind is with me

Empty the boat, lighten the load, and sail swiftly

anchorite

swimming for dear life

away from the shipwreck of society

digging into desert

lodging fast:

like the holdfast

from which kelp extends

a floating bulb and blades:

its smallest part

glued to rock

hooked into place:

does the opened heart

attached, anchored—unleash hope?

that buoyant annual

Master your hands and your feet, your words and your thoughts

Mountain pose

You feel it's just standstill.

Stopped, what are you doing?

Inhale.

Breath earth-worming.

Feet rooting.

Outside, a tussle of dogs barking.

Blackberries bloom on the bank.

Exhale.

The sacrum drops, floating ribs rise.

Space drifts into the spine,

entering your reservations.

Flesh at the edge of mind's light-well

tingles, bells as it hollows.

Chest with drawers ajar.

Stuff caught, hanging out.

Gnatlight glazing evening leaves.

The southlands in tears.

You have crossed a great body of water

and pause on its further shore,

looking backwards and forwards.

Waves. A racket of pebbles as the beach drains.

Standing backbend

Sweep the arms up
in a wheel of wings.
Remember rain's trails to the underworld?
Penumbra of purple under your heels.
Unbutton your heavy overcoat.
Mind climbs the narrow staircase of the spine
and opens a door on the landing.
Autumn has flushed the plump apples overhead.
Wind soft as a fox's tail
brushes your skin. You rise
like warmth from a fire
and curl over the orchard,
look back, look down.

Standing forward bend

Eyes follow the procession

of your hands as you exhale and swing them

down to the ground: a narrow road from summit-top

to salt stones. A fresh wind.

Let mud-ball head swing free,

fold belly over a clothesline,

and ignore the prison wall scratched

up the backs of your legs.

Planting rice without a hat.

Breath blows its long horns through your bones

into the whorls of fingerprints.

This is a small offering

in harmony with the time.

The heart at rest is a moonstone.

Lunge

When the hero came to the inn

under drooping willows,

he dug between their roots and found the spring.

In the light of the setting sun,

he could see the golden mountain.

Jasmine hung so thickly above the kitchen door

he had to stoop, going in to the fire.

Its light guttered and flared, striking the hard table.

A man and a child looked up, wondering why he'd come.

He recalled the window seat

and his absorption, moving lines of pawns

through slanted beams of light.

Later, he'd herded cows.

The king had used him

to snare the followers who'd pleaded for their lives.

Thunder dogged his heels after he escaped the city.

For himself, he did not mind if death came early or late.

Unlacing his boots, he set them on the hearth.

Plank pose

Earth-smoke as evening
banks the sun, closing its vault.
Tall foam-tuft fumitory, small bleeding heart.
In the darkening, Joseph on a donkey
holds the little he knows and heads for Egypt.

Finding your arms. Finding
the discipline of flatness.

Afloat while legions of minutes—
time's corpuscles in the preponderant void—
run through visiting hours, Chinese water torture,
and collect in the ladle of a single gesture.
Shocked by night's crowded ocean of gods,
you find in yourself the practice of a log
riding out waves of darkness.

Downstairs, in front of the fire,
a child is clearing the table.
Spikes of delphiniums hit by a storm
hover close to the ground.

Dip, eight parts pose

Exhaling,
dip your chin and chest
to the floor.
Eight points touch ground:
feet, knees, hands, chest, chin.

Revolution.
A ganglion of lightning
igniting the lake with white wings. Don't die
though death knocks hard
on the creaking door
this hour. Our delusions won't breed
more goods, gold, food.
Yogis say the eight-fold way
will summon blessings. A magician
is a calendar-maker.
Crushed and crumpled pages,
the course of sweet bohemias antiquated,
even shoe leather in disgrace—
bow like a tiger and drink
lake water tingling with fire.

How will you become free?

Like hundreds of leathery white eggs laid in a grave,
all the universes spawned by Ananta, Lord of the Serpents—
all their mountains, cliffs, torrents, all they'll become—
supported by coils of gravity. And in our bodies,
the microcosm buried at the base of the spine.
Asanas a ladder, tunes it can climb. Chakra after chakra
lighting up, luminous hood reaching over the crown—
greeting one a long-ago poet named his Lord
of the Meeting Rivers, and another poet, the one
who cast off her clothes, called my Lord White as Jasmine.

How gladly you follow the words of the awakened

These need eating, tout suite!
Handwritten on a scrap of paper torn from a sheet
and placed under a softening peach, the last
and, no doubt, furthest gone: brown
breaking down the cream under its skin,
a tang—on the edge of turning—but, oh…
sweet and loaded, intensely a peach,
more so since the mouth could tell that soon
fermentation would spread, the fruit would melt
into something inedible.

When a truth becomes urgent,
why wouldn't a person in any time, people in many places,
recognize it and tell us—so this bit wouldn't sink again
into oblivion, but be known in the form it had taken?
The way light every day reveals what's living with us
in our time's tiny pocket, as if we could sense its beauty, quit
jingling coins and fingering lint, feel tender, be intimate.
And in the end, of course, it would only be a peach—
not a tree nor a moon, not a horse—neither a galaxy
nor a universe. Just a fruit that got eaten.
These need eating, tout suite!

Hold your tongue

Ich habe genug.
I do. I have enough.
And have had enough.

In a wood of slender trees
poplar leaves twirl.
Glade distended with milky light.

Her voice, poured from a blue jug,
could be the wind
but it's more loosey-goosey, full hipped.

Schlummert ein, ihr matten Augen.
Filling us with promise. Time and again,
pain ends. *Ich habe genug.*

Look within—the rising and the falling

the inner eye
while practicing asanas
turning out hip sockets
emptying the walking sticks of femurs into its palms
rotating their noggins—

the little eye on its fine tube
trained in pranayama
to probe airways: lung's tennis court
jammed with pup tents—note taut rows
neatly inflated—then saggy, sleepy rows—
and even the abandoned bundles
under the collarbones—that little working eye recording
findings, reel after reel of documentation—
the little everyday eye following the breath,
watching as troops head out on many trails—turning up
for a rescue: scrambling onto the edge of pain, watching
breath throw out a line, haul the injured up to a stretcher,
tuck her under a blanket, give sips of tea from a thermos—
the little eye by her side, taking her hand—

yes, the little eye

on long holdings withdrawn

to the map room, to the charts it can unroll

across the navigator's table to pinpoint a channel

sounded one rainy afternoon—the eye sketching a route,

persuaded by a visiting yogi that there's a fine blue passage

running from inner ear to lower brain,

down through vertebrae (five, six, seven),

branching out to an iris on the shoulder blade,

down arm, across elbow, out thumb—

a thread like an embroidery yarn, each stitch visible—

an eye willing to see blue lines and red lines

like wiring inside the skin, an eye

like a hydroelectrician bent on lighting up a plant—

and at rest,

the closing eye's drooping gaze

sliding down the nose like ghee, a fat drop at its tip,

falling into the soup, watching while not watching

the pot as tiny bubbles creep up the side

and something circulates, perhaps a chunk of carrot—

feeling the gaze spread wider, glaze over

until things extend into their reflections

and light dissolves all density—

the eye dropped like a strand of egg white

into stock, turning over,

tumbling into threads—blindly collecting what's opaque,

withdrawing it—at work even when

at rest: yes, that

eye

clarifying

By your own efforts, waken yourself, watch yourself

here, the air is visible
each particle carries
a mirror of water

spruce needles
ferret out beads of moisture,
collect a delicate rain
for their dry roots

elsewhere, the sky is clear,
the day warm—
bees keep busy, cats loll in the sun—
but this fog
is not moved: it holds its seat

the air gathers more lumen—
its mirrors coated with mother-of-pearl:
breath's lustre—
as if the usually transparent atmosphere
sat brooding
on its acumen, hour after hour

determined to see itself

to memorize

its features so that when it gets up,

stretches, and begins to act

it will not forget itself

Do not exult yourself

After Mahādēviyakka 11

Between ocean and cloud, a fog is moving:
milk in the air's currents.

Swan's down along curls of breeze
to feather the branches of trees.

They say a swan
can part milk from water

and one cannot tell which came before
and which after.

Suckled by gods, even an ant could grow
as galaxies grow—demonic.

How sweet to be free

the bees come and go, feeding on fireweed
below them, fog rolls in and out, blanketing
beaches, rumpling over lower slopes
above them, contrails
like sagging streamers after a party
but here, an alpine clarity in the air
and the sun's gaze day after day
like a mother keeping her eye on her brood
as they swing, climb, balance, race

to fulfill the promise
of the fourth age, sages say
one may hide away—in a desert,
in a forest, in a cell—and busy oneself
with a ceaseless longing

Make it your own

What if a name
bestowed character? Became itself—
as does an iris taking on
hazel or grey or green or brown
precipitated from a newborn's navy blue—
by hauling in a mysterious anchor,
stowing in the namesake's locker
wet coils connected to other sea bottoms,
to flanges that cut under anemones,
cast shells, tilted rock?
                    What if a name
carried, encoded in its voicing,
links to other speakers
who spoke it—scathingly, urgently—
calling it out in woods and hearing it
shoulder through leaves,
hurrying, hurrying to the one
within hailing distance?
                    Or the murmur
when a lover turns his head, lips
no longer on her lips,
sighing her name?
                    Subtle signature—
a mitochondria of usage—is this how
a word knows so much?

For see how the jasmine releases and lets fall its withered flowers

The clutter and clatter
of what I drag
along behind me—a dilapidated cart
rocking on its wooden wheels
over roots
and rubble on a track
through second-growth alder, wind-bent spruce,
past trail-side mounds of sharp-edged grass
habituated to salt air,
splay of knotted ropes
pulling chairs, bedsteads, tables, hutches,
even an overflowing Turkish han—market and caravansary—
like a tottering museum piece, oozing smoke, spilling
tears and grain and silk-wrapped books, stinking
of saddles and piss-pots in its corners
and, trailing after this rattletrap,
the silent child
with her kites of longing, their shard-coated cords
slicing each other, paper fishes
drifting off to clouds—no wonder
it takes such energy
to get going:
can I not
emerge from the past's brown days, leave them

dropped here, to decay
with toppled trees and fallen branches, overtaken
by salal and coated with moss, and walk
quietly and freely on my way?

Like the moon, come out from behind the clouds. Shine!

After Mahādēviyakka 131

Dawn. November. Long, lucid guard hairs

on the mackerel coat of strait and sky.

As light brightens the grey, one remnant

in the bay: a lock of dark strands—

as if she'd drowned;

as if the strait's

frigid current slid against her skull, lifted

the tresses she dressed herself in, spread them out

tugging slightly

so her naked body swayed

like a kelp stalk held fast

to an underwater outcrop of pillow basalt.

As if a hollow stem

gelled in bitter water, growing sixty feet

last summer—bulb afloat, blades aswirl—were rootless

but for a small fist of vacanas—

                lyrics she spoke in an argument

            with Allama, master of the mansion of experience

                          nine centuries ago—

                  gripping silks of sunlight daylong

                    layering leaves licking wind

                      six colours aflicker creepers

                              lush trysts

                                        in which

                                    she forgot herself

                                 sought him—her lord

                                  white as jasmine—

                        her words drowned in the long night.

A flock of cormorants,

skimming

grey waves, arrows off.

To think her—aslant

sinuous, luminous—in this day, in this bay.

Live in love. Do your work. Make an end of your sorrows.

and now the rains
have come
sword fern frond bent down
collecting water along its seam
reflecting sky

its curved track
supposing something not a train
to whoosh down its back: something
that could slide (playful, lonely)—something
with feet, wing beat, the drive
of intuition—nothing to buy tickets for: no
holiday bird

such loveliness and sorrow
as if one saw
all the lost species: horses the size of dogs
then rocks in freeze-frame, hoisting themselves
into mountains—a fairground of galaxies,
carousels of stars—spun inside out until presently
this formless one, sentenced
to turn over every stone, searching
for anything that could be
a soul mate, checking stuff out by making

love recklessly and tenderly—its craving patient and fresh
puddle on gravel
pocked with falling drops, filled
with something out of nowhere
sinking slowly in

for now the rains
have come

Notes & Acknowledgements

Notes

The epigraph is from Roo Borson, "Autumn Record," *Short Journey Upriver Toward Oishida*, Toronto: McClelland & Stewart, 2004.

Active Pass

Prior to European contact, Cowichan women kept small dogs whose fleece was sheared off with a mussel shell knife, mixed with mountain goat wool and goose down, and woven with cedar bark into blankets. These dogs became extinct around the time of the gold rush (1860s). In my childhood, Cowichan women knit highly-prized sweaters. I was told that these were wonderfully waterproof and warm because of dog fur, collected from mongrels on the reservation, in the yarn. My father claimed you could smell the dog in his sweater when it got wet. I sniffed but wasn't sure; still, I liked the idea that their dogs helped the Cowichan women make a living.

Nursery rhymes helped shape these poems. "Peter, Peter Pumpkin-Eater / Had a wife and couldn't keep her. / Put her in a pumpkin shell / And there he kept her very well" may be more familiar than one of my favourites: "Old Mother Goose, when she wanted to wander / Would ride through the air on a very fine gander." Both spoke to tensions associated with working away from home.

Once, I heard of a shaman or spirit woman named Shu'ua, probably on the radio. What I remember is my dream about her, not the story that prompted it. The Songhees (from the southern end of Vancouver Island) did have a type of shaman called a *si'oua* who was usually a woman. Her function was to appease hostile powers, to whom she spoke a sacred language. Women applied to her if they desired children or wanted other kinds of charms.

Mary Pratt: Illuminations

The quotation under the title for this section comes from Mary Pratt, *A Personal Calligraphy,* Fredericton: Goose Lane Editions, 2000.

I also am grateful for Tom Smart, *The Art of Mary Pratt: The Substance of Light*, Fredericton: Goose Lane Editions and The Beaverbrook Art Gallery, 1995, and for *Simple Bliss: the paintings and prints of Mary Pratt*, Patricia Deadman, curator, and Robin Laurence, guest writer, Regina: MacKenzie Art Gallery, 2004, for reproductions of her paintings and woodblock prints, and details about her life and work.

Apart from the first and last, the poems in the second section are titled after Mary Pratt's paintings.

Tsimshian nax nox dancer—*nax nox* are spiritual powers or supernatural forces. In the nesting pair of prehistoric granite nax nox masks that were reunited in a 1965 exhibition originating at the Art Gallery of Greater Victoria, the inner mask has its eyes open and the outer mask has its eyes closed. We're used to seeing masks made of lighter materials. Not only did an artist carve these haunting twins, but a dancer bore the weight of both—looking out and looking in—when performing at a feast or potlatch. Another tidbit: masks are particularly associated with matrilineal cultures.

Both Mary and Christopher Pratt worked from photographic slides. They each painted portraits of Donna Meaney, first Christopher, and then—more candidly—Mary. She commonly used photographic sources, adapting and transforming the image as she worked. When painting Donna, she began with 35-mm slides taken by her husband of his model looking at him. Mary also used photographs to record her exploration and completion of a painting.

Nearer Prayer than Story

The title for the third section alludes to something John Berger says in *and our faces, my heart, brief as photos*. The full quotation is "Poems are nearer to prayers than to stories, but in poetry there is no one behind the language being prayed to." (London: Bloomsbury Publishing, 1984/2005)

The titles for poems in the third section are drawn from chapter 25, "The Seeker," of the *Dhammapada: The Sayings of the Buddha* as rendered by Thomas Byrom in the Shambhala edition, 1993.

The "Whale Étude" is a painting by Vancouver artist, Ranjan Sen.

Bach's "Ich habe genug" (I have enough), Cantata BWV 82, was recorded by Lorraine Hunt Lieberson in 2002 while she was battling terminal breast cancer. The second aria of this cantata is the lullaby, "Schlummert ein, ihr matten Augen," which can be translated as "Slumber now, you tired eyes." Originally, this whole cantata was composed for a man's voice because it was Simeon's song—the prophet in the temple who recognized the infant Jesus as the Lord's Messiah and said he could now die in peace, having seen the promised one. "My eyes have seen your salvation..." (Luke 22-35). The closing eyes in Bach's lullaby aria refer to Simeon's sense of freedom and fulfillment. But, in German, *ich habe genug* means both "I've had enough" and "I have enough." In English, "I have had enough" is something one might say about bad behaviour—or, about enduring pain and suffering. Lieberson's rendition of the cantata conveys its complexity of emotional and spiritual meanings, and even the echo of Simeon. I imagined her singing it in the woods tended by a Benedictine hermit, James Gray, who always claimed he was ready to die though he loved life and the land he knew so well.

Mahādēviyakka (archetypal elder sister of all souls) was a twelfth-century poet from the south of India who composed vacanas (free-verse lyrics) in Kannada, her vernacular. The numbers in my subtitles refer to English translations of her poems by A.K. Ramanujan, *Speaking of Siva*, New York: Penguin, 1973. Mahādēviyakka, while informed by traditional Sanskrit poetry, drew imagery from the outdoors, village life and her personal relationships. She was the only woman accepted into a college of bhakti saints—yogic philosophers and poets. As a form of protest, she refused to wear clothing, covering herself only with her hair.

Acknowledgements

Many of these poems have been published, sometimes in earlier versions, in the following journals: *The Antigonish Review, The Fiddlehead, Literary Review of Canada, North American Maple: A Literary Journal, Prairie Fire, Prism International* and *The Warwick Review.* "Do not exult yourself: after Mahadeviyakka 11" and "Like the moon, come out from behind the clouds. Shine!: after Mahadeviyakka 131" appeared in *Regreen: New Canadian Ecological Poetry*, Madhur Anand and Adam Dickinson (editors), Sudbury: Your Scrivener Press, 2009. "I develop a technique for unlocking doors one-handed," appeared in *Rocksalt: An Anthology of Contemporary BC Poetry* edited by Harold Rhenisch and Mona Fertig, Fulford-Ganges: Mother Tongue Publishing Limited, 2008.

An earlier version of "Active Pass" was short-listed for the 2006 CBC Literary Award.

"Master your hands and your feet, your words and your thoughts" won the 2007 Banff Centre Bliss Carman Poetry Award.

"Entering Active Pass" was Poem of the Week on the Parliamentary Poet Laureate's website, www.parl.gc.ca/poet, July 2007.

The generous support of the Canada Council for the Arts and the British Columbia Arts Council helped make this work possible.

I would also like to thank the Saskatchewan Writers' Guild for subsidizing my stays at the Writers'/Artists Colony. Many of the poems in this book began during those retreats; thanks to my fellow colonists and the community at St. Peter's Abbey. I am grateful to the yoga teachers who guide my practice: Shirley Daventry French and others at the Iyengar Yoga Centre of Victoria. And, thanks to Queenswood in Victoria for accommodating me and my writing on day retreats.

This book owes much to the love of friends and family. In particular, I would like to thank Bob Amussen, Roo Borson, Jan Conn, Lorna Crozier, Becky Helfer and Ian Munro for their listening, reading and encouragement. Special thanks go to Jan Zwicky for her enthusiastic and insightful responses to the poems, and for our many conversations.

Active Pass is dedicated to Roo Borson who has seen me through and through decades of straits and narrows, including the "active pass" that gave rise to these poems.

★ ★ ★

JANE MUNRO lives on Vancouver Island BC. Previous works of poetry include:

Point No Point, McClelland & Stewart, 2006
Grief Notes & Animal Dreams, Brick Books, 1995
The Trees Just Moved Into A Season Of Other Shapes,
    Quarry Press, 1986
Daughters, Fiddlehead Poetry Books: Fredericton, NB, 1982